Contents

What is a flood?

A flood occurs when a large amount of water covers land that is usually dry. Heavy rain and storms can cause flooding, **mudslides** and **landslides**. Stormy weather can also whip up big waves that crash over the shore, covering the land in water.

▶ People in Villahermosa in Mexico had to flee their homes in October 2007 after floods swept the city.

Angela Royston

Wild Weather
FLOODS

QED

Copyright © QED Publishing 2008
First published in the UK in 2008 by
QED Publishing
A Quarto Group Company
226 City Road
London EC1V 2TT
www.qed-publishing.co.uk

A catalogue record for this book is available from the British Library.

ISBN 978 1 84835 072 4

Printed and bound in China

Author Angela Royston
Consultant Terry Jennings
Editor Amanda Askew
Designer Mo Choy
Picture Researcher Claudia Tate
Illustrator Julian Baker

Publisher Steve Evans
Creative Director Zeta Davies

Picture credits (a=above, b=below)
Alamy 27a Vera Schimetzek, 27b Jon Arnold Images Ltd

Corbis 5a Kelly Owen/ZUMA, 5b Gideon Mendel, 6b Jon Hicks, 11a Gideon Mendel, 14 Anatoly Maltsev/epa, 17a Smiley N Pool/Dallas Morning News, 19b Romeo Ranoco/Reuters, 20b Reuters, 26 Louie Psihoyos, 29 Paul Souders

Getty Images 1 Kevin Horan, 4 AFP, 8b, 10 AFP, 12, 13a Steve Coleman, 15a, 15b AFP, 16, 17b Peter Timmermans, 19a, 21, 23b Tim Graham

Science Photo Library 7a Gary Hincks, 9b Garry D McMichael, 11b Gary Hincks

Shutterstock 6a Stephen Strathdee, 8a MaxFX, 13b Celso Diniz, 18 Ronfromyork, 20a Jerry Sharp, 22 Karen Hadley, 23a Diana Lundin, 24 Paul Vorwerk, 25a Puchan, 25b Palis Michael

Words in **bold** can be found in the glossary on page 30.

WHY DOES FLOODING OCCUR?

When there is heavy rain, more water than usual flows into rivers, often causing the rivers to overflow. This is the most common cause of flooding and has a particularly disastrous effect if the river runs through a town or city. Lakes and even the sea can overflow, too.

▼ **Meteorologists** try to predict the weather so that people can prepare for heavy rainfall and other extreme weather.

WHAT ARE THE EFFECTS OF A FLOOD?

Floods can ruin homes and destroy farm crops. In severe cases, people may drown. Flood water may cover buildings, wash away bridges and roads, and disrupt electricity and other supplies. Mud, litter and waste is washed everywhere. In towns and cities, waste water from streets and buildings drains into sewers. If there is too much water for the drains to hold, the dirty water flows back up the drains, so flood water is often contaminated with **sewage**.

▶ In June 2007, a freak storm flooded the village of Rotherham, England. People had to be rescued by dingy boat.

What causes rain?

Clouds are made of tiny droplets of water. When cooled, they can join together to make bigger drops. When the drops become too heavy, they fall to the ground as rain.

HEAVY RAIN

The heaviest downpours of rain come from huge black clouds called **cumulonimbus**. They form when warm, moist air rises quickly. The air tumbles around inside the cloud. This is called turbulence and makes the clouds look as though they are boiling. The turbulence pushes the water droplets around these huge clouds, causing them to crash into each other and form larger drops.

▲ Cumulonimbus clouds often form in summer. They are a sure sign of very heavy rain and perhaps a thunderstorm, too.

▼ A thunderstorm brings heavy rain to Johannesburg, South Africa.

THE WATER CYCLE

As the Sun heats the Earth, water from the surface of the oceans, lakes and rivers **evaporates** – the water becomes a gas called water vapour and floats into the air. As the vapour rises, it cools and **condenses** – becomes water again – into tiny water droplets, which form clouds. The rain from these clouds falls on the land and soaks into the ground or runs into streams, rivers and lakes. Most rivers flow into the ocean, where the water may evaporate and the cycle begins again.

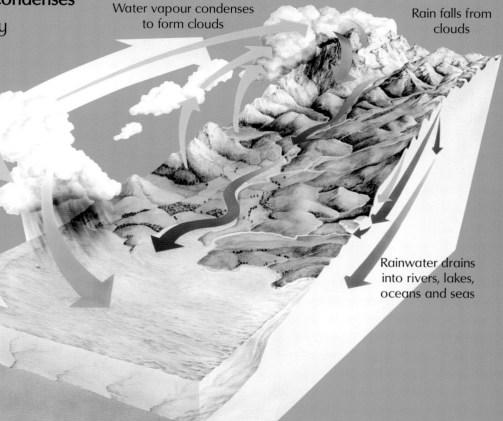

Water vapour condenses to form clouds

Rain falls from clouds

Water evaporates into the air

Rainwater drains into rivers, lakes, oceans and seas

▶ Water moves between the oceans, seas, air and land in a continuous cycle called the water cycle.

HEAVY RAIN

Short bursts of heavy rain can happen almost anywhere in the world. On 3 July 1975, more than 40 centimetres of rain fell in one hour in Shangdi, China.

which places get the most rain?

It rains almost every day in some places on or near the **Equator**. Deserts, however, get almost no rain at all. The kind of weather a place usually gets is called its climate.

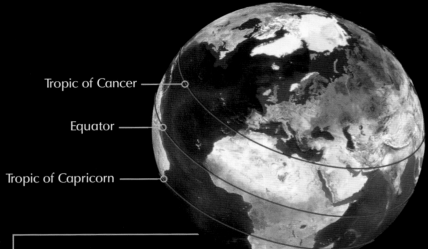

Tropic of Cancer
Equator
Tropic of Capricorn

▲ The **tropics** are the hottest places on Earth. They lie between the tropic of Cancer and the tropic of Capricorn.

▼ This village in southern Bangladesh was flooded when a **cyclone** hit the country in 2007.

WET CLIMATES

Places are often wet where the wind blows from the ocean onto the land. Winds bring rain from the Atlantic Ocean, for example, to the west coast of the British Isles. Some tropical areas are very wet. The heat of the Sun is strongest along the Equator, so more water evaporates from the ocean, creating heavy rain when the clouds blow over the land. **Monsoons** are winds that carry this rain over the land. They blow for part of the year, bringing a rainy season to some countries. In India, for example, the monsoon wind brings heavy rainfall from June to September.

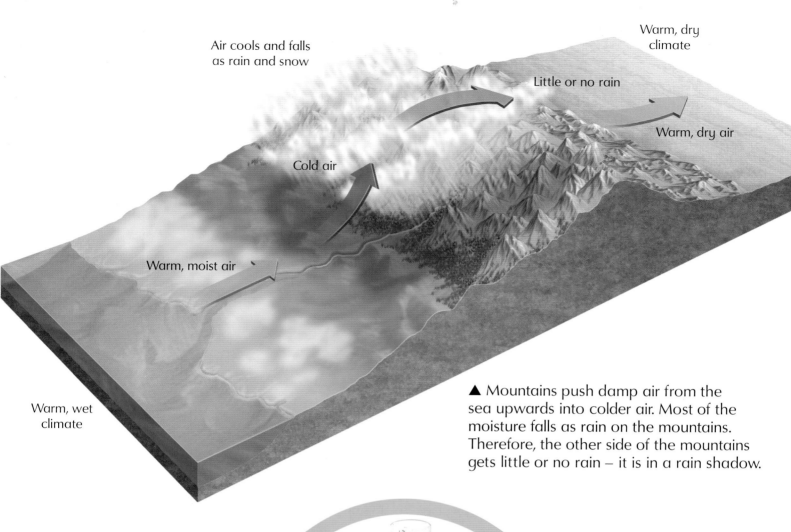

Air cools and falls
as rain and snow

Warm, dry
climate

Little or no rain

Warm, dry air

Cold air

Warm, moist air

Warm, wet
climate

▲ Mountains push damp air from the
sea upwards into colder air. Most of the
moisture falls as rain on the mountains.
Therefore, the other side of the mountains
gets little or no rain – it is in a rain shadow.

RAIN SHADOW

When winds blow
moist air against high
mountains, the air is
forced upwards. As
the rising air cools, the
moisture condenses and
falls on the mountainside
as rain. The other side of
the mountain may get almost
no rain at all. This is called a
rain shadow. On the Hawaiian island
of Kauai, Mount Waialeale blocks rain clouds
coming from the Pacific Ocean. The side that
faces the ocean has one of the wettest climates
in the world, with 1170 centimetres of rain a
year, but the other side is dry.

◄ A rain gauge is read at
the same time each day
so that one day can be
compared with another.

MEASURING RAIN

Meteorologists are
scientists who study and
forecast the weather. They use
rain gauges to measure rainfall.
The amount of rain that falls in
24 hours is measured each day,
eventually giving the yearly,
or annual, rainfall.

Flooding rivers

River floods are usually caused by heavy rain. When rain falls for many weeks, the ground becomes so wet that rain cannot soak into it. The extra water drains into streams and rivers, which can cause them to overflow. Floods can also be caused by melting snow draining into rivers.

MISSISSIPPI-MISSOURI FLOOD

In 1993, heavy rain caused flooding along the Mississippi and Missouri rivers in the USA. Towns were flooded and 10,000 homes were destroyed. In the city of St Louis, where the rivers meet, some places remained underwater for 200 days. The flooding caused $20 billion (£10 billion) worth of damage and is often called the Great Flood.

RISING WATER

A flood can take weeks to build up. The river water level rises and, in places, the water flows faster. Fast-flowing water creates a strong force that can wash away trees and bridges. Bridges are often built where the river is narrowest. The water can then become stuck and the level rises even more.

◄ People had to use canoes and other boats to go from house to house on land covered by the Mississippi-Missouri flood.

WHERE DO RIVERS FORM?

Rivers begin in mountains and hills. Streams join together to make a river, which then flows through the valley into the sea. After heavy rain, many rivers overflow their banks onto the low-lying land beside the river, called a **floodplain**.

When there is too much extra water, the floodplain cannot take any more and nearby farmland, towns and cities are flooded.

▲ When the Severn River in England burst its banks in 2007, it flooded the surrounding land. The long line of trees shows where the river normally flows.

Source

◄ Water always flows downhill from mountains and hills to lower, flatter ground and then into the sea.

Delta

Floodplain

River mouth

Flash floods

Many floods take several days or weeks to build up, but flash floods can form in just a few hours. A heavy downpour of rain in one place quickly fills **gorges** and valleys. Some flash floods occur in deserts – the last place you might expect a flood.

▲ The streets became rivers in Boscastle in Cornwall, England, in the summer of 2004. Much of the damage was caused by trees and other debris that were swept along with the water.

VALLEYS

Flash floods are most likely to occur in summer, when the Sun's heat creates big thunderclouds. In August 2004, a seaside town of Boscastle, Cornwall, England, was hit by heavy rain that lasted several hours. The town is at the bottom of a steep valley. Water poured down the valley and through the town. It flooded homes and swept many cars into the harbour.

▲ When the Namibian Desert in southern Africa floods, the water quickly soaks into the ground.

▶ **Dams**, such as the Hoover Dam in Colorado, USA, help to prevent floods by controlling the flow of water through them.

BURSTING DAMS

A dam is a wall built across a valley to block a river. It stores the water and often generates electricity, too. If the lake behind the dam becomes too full, the weight of water can burst the wall. Then billions of tonnes of water flood the area. In February 2005, the Shadikor Dam in Pakistan burst, killing at least 60 people and sweeping away five villages.

DESERTS

In a desert, flash floods usually begin with a thunderstorm and heavy rain. The ground is so dry and hard, the rainwater cannot soak in. Instead, it pours into **riverbeds** that are usually dry. The riverbed quickly becomes full of rushing water. Flash floods can begin in mountains far away, so they arrive without warning. The first sign may be the roar of the approaching wall of water, giving people little time to climb to safety on higher ground. Flash floods can hit cities, too. In August 2003, thunderstorms in the Southwest Desert, USA, produced heavy rain that flooded part of Las Vegas. Two people were killed and many motorists became trapped.

Mudslides

Heavy rain can cause landslides and mudslides on steep slopes. In a landslide, the water loosens part of the hillside so that rocks, trees and boulders begin to slip downhill. In a mudslide, liquid mud pours down the slope.

▶ In September 2002, this huge landslide blocked the Karmadon Gorge in Russia.

CAUSES OF MUDSLIDES

Mudslides are most likely to occur on slopes where the trees have been cut down or burned in a **wildfire**. Tree roots hold the soil in place, so without them, the soil becomes loose and unstable. In heavy rain, the water mixes with the soil, which turns it into a liquid that can flow at speeds of up to 100 kilometres an hour.

◄ Heavy rains in California, USA, in April 2006 caused a mudslide. Rescuers worked to free two people trapped in their home.

SUFFOCATING MUD

Landslides and mudslides block roads and trap people. Rescuing people can be difficult because the area is often hard to reach and the land is unstable. In October 2005, heavy rain from a **hurricane** triggered a mudslide that completely covered the village of Panabaj, Guatemala. In some places, the mud was 4 to 6 metres in depth. Rescuers used dogs to search for victims, but 400 people were never found.

▼ Search and rescue teams look for survivors after Guinsaugon, Leyte, was destroyed by a mudslide.

LEYTE, PHILIPPINES

In February 2006, a mudslide covered the mountain village of Guinsaugon on the island of Leyte in the Philippines. It is estimated that 200 people died and a further 1500 people were never found.

Sea floods

Sometimes the sea floods land. Storms create huge waves that crash onto the coast, but storms do the most damage at **high tide** because then the wind easily blows extra water onto the shore. Seawater can flood low-lying land, coastal towns and villages.

TSUNAMIS
A tsunami can cause devastating sea floods. A tsunami is not caused by wild weather, however, but by an earthquake in the seabed. Huge waves hit the shore, flooding land along the coast.

▼ During a storm in November 2007, the sea wall in Lowestoft, England, was not high enough to hold back the waves at high tide.

HURRICANES

Hurricanes are tropical storms that begin over the ocean. They can create a **storm surge** – a bulge in the sea several metres high. This is higher than most shorelines. When the storm reaches land, the storm surge hits the coast and floods beyond the shore. High sea walls are built to keep out the waves. In August 2005, Hurricane Katrina hit New Orleans, USA. Protective walls called **levees** collapsed and the storm surge swept into the city, flooding 80 percent of it.

▲ Many homes in New Orleans, USA, were almost completely covered by flood water following Hurricane Katrina.

▲ In the Netherlands, wind pumps help to keep the land drained of water.

LOW-LYING LAND

There is a higher risk of flooding for land that is not far above the level of the sea. Bangladesh often floods during the rainy season because extra water in the Ganges River overflows onto the low-lying land. If a storm hits the coast, water floods onto the land from the river and the sea. In some places, such as the Netherlands, the land is actually lower than the sea. Here, the land has been **reclaimed** from the sea. The water is held back by strong walls called **dykes**, and the low-lying land is built up, using soil and rocks, to a height that is less likely to flood.

Preparing for floods

Flash floods can happen without warning, but many floods can be predicted. River floods can build up over several days. Meteorologists track hurricanes and try to predict where they will hit land and how strong they will be.

▼ Sandbags are used to build a wall, keeping out flood water for a short time.

PREPARING FOR RIVER FLOODS

People who live close to rivers are most at risk of flooding. Local authorities use radio and television to warn people if they think a flood is likely. Sandbags are placed at the bottom of doorways to keep the water out, and valuable items are moved to higher floors. As the flood becomes more certain, electricity and gas supplies are turned off. Some people may have to leave their homes altogether and go to shelters that have been set up further away from the river.

PREPARING FOR COASTAL FLOODS

It is difficult for meteorologists to predict exactly where a hurricane is likely to hit the coast. Many people prepare for the worst. They may buy in supplies of food and drinking water. As a hurricane gets nearer to a particular area, people are advised to leave the coast and move inland. **Evacuation** can take hours, as thousands of cars and other vehicles jam the roads.

▲ In October 2005, a flood shelter was set up in Taunton, Massachusetts, USA, when the authorities were worried that a nearby dam might burst.

EVACUATION

When a hurricane or river flood is expected, people who are likely to be badly affected get ready to leave their homes. People watch television or listen to the radio. When they are advised to evacuate their homes, they pack what they will need and travel inland or up to higher ground. Many people stay with friends or family. Other people go to flood shelters that the local authorities have organized, usually in schools, church halls or sports stadiums. The shelters provide beds, blankets and food until the flood is over.

▶ Filipino people walk to safety after their homes were flooded by a **typhoon**.

Destructive power of water

Flood water can block roads, destroy bridges and wash away cars and buildings. Even if people have been warned that there is risk of flooding, they may be taken by surprise. Flood water can rise quickly, trapping people in their homes or cars.

RESCUE OPERATIONS

Sandbags can keep water out, but only for a while. As the level rises, the water eventually seeps through. If the lower floor of a house fills with water, people have to go up to a higher floor. If the flood keeps rising, they may climb out onto the roof. In a town or village, rescuers may be able to reach stranded people by boat. If they cannot, helicopters lift people to safety.

▲ If flood water brings down a bridge, cars can be washed into the river.

◀ A helicopter rescues a woman from a building by the Limpopo River in Mozambique.

LARGE-SCALE FLOODING

If flooding covers a large area, millions of people can be affected. In November 2007, heavy rain flooded much of the state of Tabasco, Mexico. About 500,000 people were made homeless and millions were without electricity or clean water. When an electricity **power station** is flooded, the electricity supply can be cut for weeks. When electricity fails, water can no longer be pumped to towns and homes and, if the **water purification system** is flooded, the water supply has to be stopped.

WILDLIFE

Animals are also affected by floods. Where possible, farm animals are taken to higher ground, but wild animals have to look after themselves. Unless they can swim or get to higher ground in time, many smaller animals drown.

◀ In 2007, flood water surrounded the town of Tewkesbury, England, turning it into an island.

Repairing the damage

Once flood water has drained away, the repair work can begin – on damaged roads and bridges, and cleaning up buildings. Fire crews pump water out of basements, cellars and other places where it may be trapped.

▼ During a flood, roads can be damaged and washed away.

INSIDE HOMES

Even shallow water can cause damage in a home. Flood water is dirty and often contaminated with sewage. Everything it covers becomes filthy. Carpets, floorboards and walls become soaked. Wooden doors and cupboards bend when they are very wet, which means that they no longer shut. Water can make metal rust or corrode, ruining plugs and sockets. Gas pipes can also be damaged by flooding. Before work can start, the house has to be checked by experts to make sure it is safe.

▲ When flood water drains away, it leaves behind a layer of filth.

▼ Fire crews not only help to rescue people during a flood, they pump out water from flooded places.

CLEANING UP

When people return after a flood, they often find their homes have been ruined. Most of the furniture, carpets and electrical goods that have been covered by water have to be thrown away. Electrical goods, such as televisions, refrigerators and washing machines, that have been underwater no longer work. Machines called dehumidifiers are used to dry the walls, floors and ceilings, but it can take months, sometimes years, before a building is completely dry and ready to be lived in again. Three years after Hurricane Katrina flooded New Orleans, USA, many people were still unable to return to their home.

Preventing floods

One way to prevent floods is to build barriers to stop river water and the sea from flooding the land. Another is to preserve trees and natural marshes, which soak up extra water. However, it is best not to build on land that is likely to flood.

FLOOD BARRIERS

The easiest way to stop a river flooding is to build a levee, which makes the riverbank higher. However, if the levee holds, it may just move the flood further downstream. Another way is to build an overflow ditch, called a **culvert**, alongside the river. After the 2004 flood in Boscastle, Cornwall, England, a culvert was built. When heavy rain hit the town again in 2007, flood water was diverted into the culvert and the town was saved from severe damage.

NATURAL WETLAND

Water meadows are grassy fields alongside riverbanks. **Salt marshes** and mangrove swamps are **wetlands** alongside the coast. They act like natural sponges soaking up and storing extra water. One reason that floods have increased in many countries, including the UK, is that many wetlands have been drained and new homes built on them.

▼ The Thames Barrier in London, England, stops seawater coming up the river when the tide is extra high or when wind pushes extra water inland.

▲ Water meadows regularly flood with water when the river is full.

DEFORESTATION

Many forests are being cut down, either to sell the wood or make farmland. Trees take up large amounts of water through their roots and are particularly important on mountainsides and hillsides. When trees are cut down, the water runs downhill into the rivers, making mudslides and floods more likely.

▼ Wildfires have destroyed all the trees on this hillside, making a mudslide more likely.

Living with floods

Today, many people are living in areas that are likely to flood. Some architects are beginning to design and build new homes that can survive a flood, but these houses are expensive.

▲ Rice is grown on **terraces** cut into the hillsides in Bali, Indonesia. The terraces catch the water and spread it evenly down the hill.

TAKING ADVANTAGE OF FLOODS

Rice needs plenty of water to grow, so many rice farmers plant their crops on flooded land called paddy fields. Tambaqui fish live in rivers in the Amazon rainforest, which regularly flood onto surrounding land. Then the fish swim among the trees to feed on fruit that has fallen into the water.

▼ Houses on the River Maas in the Netherlands look ordinary, but when the river rises, they rise with it.

▶ Houses are kept out of the water with stilts. The stilts are strong enough to withstand the force of the water.

KEEPING ABOVE THE WATER

For many years, people have built homes above the water or lived in floating homes, such as houseboats. In South East Asia, many traditional homes are built on **stilts**. In Lewes, England, one architect has started building modern homes on stilts. In the Netherlands, floating houses are becoming more common. The 'cellar' is full of air so that the house can float and the house is attached to two fixed poles. As the water rises, the house slides up the poles so it does not float away!

FLOOD-PROOFING

Ordinary houses can be adapted to make flooding less damaging. **Flood guards** keep out water better than sandbags because they have rubber seals to keep the water out for longer. Inside the building, tiled floors take the place of fitted carpets. Walls can also be made waterproof. Electric sockets are placed high up the walls, out of reach of shallow water, and washing machines and other electrical goods are placed on platforms above floor level. To stop sewage coming back into the house, special plugs can be pushed into the **U-bends** of waste pipes.

Are floods getting worse?

Climates around the world are changing. In the last 20 years, many places have suffered more extreme weather. The main reason for this is that the average temperature of the air is becoming warmer. This is called **global warming**.

GLOBAL WARMING

The Sun's heat is trapped in the Earth's atmosphere by **greenhouse gases**, including **carbon dioxide**. When **fossil fuels** – oil, coal and natural gas – are burned, they produce carbon dioxide, which escapes into the air. In the last 50 years, people have been burning more and more fossil fuels.

DISAPPEARING ISLANDS

Some islands in the Pacific and Indian oceans are in danger of disappearing. Much of the land on the Maldive Islands is no more than 1.5 metres above sea level. Many people have already abandoned their homes because of frequent storms and floods.

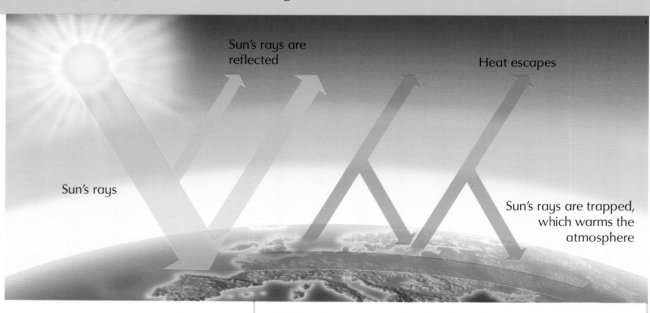

Sun's rays are reflected

Heat escapes

Sun's rays

Sun's rays are trapped, which warms the atmosphere

▲ The Sun warms the Earth and certain gases, such as carbon dioxide, trap some of the heat in the atmosphere. They act like the glass in a greenhouse.

RISING SEA LEVELS

The level of the sea is rising. Rising temperatures are melting **glaciers** and polar ice caps, pouring extra water into the oceans. As the air becomes warmer, the sea below it warms up, too. The warmer the oceans become, the more the water will expand, pushing up the level of the surface even more. Even a small increase in the level of the sea causes flooding along low-lying coasts.

▼ Glaciers are slow-moving rivers of ice. They melt in the summer sunshine. The warmer the air becomes, the faster the glaciers melt.

Glossary

CARBON DIOXIDE
One of the gases in the air. Carbon dioxide is also produced when fuel is burned.

CLOUD
A floating mass of water droplets or ice crystals.

CONDENSE
To change from a gas into a liquid.

CULVERT
A drain or channel for water. A culvert alongside a river fills when the river floods.

CUMULONIMBUS
A towering, dark cloud that often leads to heavy rain, thunderstorms and hail.

CYCLONE
A revolving tropical storm, also called a hurricane and a typhoon.

DAM
A strong wall built across a valley to block a river or stream.

DELTA
A triangular area of land and water at the mouth of a river. The land is formed by earth and sand washed down by the river.

DYKE
A high bank built to stop the sea flooding onto land.

EQUATOR
An imaginary line around the middle of the Earth, halfway between the North and South poles.

EVACUATION
Organized removal of people from a dangerous building or area.

EVAPORATE
To change from a liquid into a gas.

FLOOD GUARD
A rubber seal that is fitted over doors and air vents to keep out flood water.

FLOODPLAIN
Low, flat land alongside a river and onto which a river may often flood.

FOSSIL FUELS
Coal, oil and natural gas. These fuels were formed millions of years ago from the remains of plants and marine animals.

GLACIER
A large, slow-moving river of ice.

GLOBAL WARMING
Increase in the average temperature of the air around the Earth. Global warming is caused by an increase in greenhouse gases, such as carbon dioxide, in the air.

GORGE
A steep, narrow valley, often with a stream or river running through it.

GREENHOUSE GAS
One of the gases in the air that trap the Sun's heat. Greenhouse gases include water vapour, carbon dioxide and methane.

HIGH TIDE
When the sea comes highest up the shore. There are usually two high tides each day at any place on the coast.

HURRICANE
A violent storm with strong winds and heavy rain that begins in the Atlantic Ocean or north-east Pacific Ocean.

LANDSLIDE
A large amount of soil, rocks and plants that slides down the side of a steep slope.

LEVEE
A bank built to stop a river overflowing.

METEOROLOGIST
A scientist who studies the weather.

MONSOON
Wind in the tropics that brings weeks of heavy rain.

MUDSLIDE
Mud mixed with water that flows downhill.

POWER STATION
A building in which electricity is generated.

RECLAIMED
Recovered or returned to a state in which it can be used.

RIVERBED
A channel in the ground through which a river flows.

RIVER MOUTH
The end of a river, where it flows into a lake or the sea.

SALT MARSH
Marshy ground, often covered by salt water from the sea.

SEWAGE
Waste material and water from toilets and drains.

SOURCE
The place from which something comes. The source of a river is the place where it begins, usually on a hill or mountainside.

STILTS
Poles that raise a building above the ground.

STORM SURGE
A rapid rise in the level of the sea caused by storm winds blowing towards the shore.

TERRACES
Wide, flat steps cut into a hillside to give land for growing plants.

TROPICS
Part of the world on each side of the Equator between the Tropic of Cancer and the Tropic of Capricorn.

TYPHOON
A tropical storm that begins in the north-west Pacific Ocean and moves west, hitting countries from the Philippines to Japan.

U-BEND
U-shaped bend in a waste pipe that traps a small amount of water and stops smells coming back up the pipe.

WATER MEADOW
Flat, grassy land beside a stream or river that is flooded from time to time.

WATER PURIFICATION SYSTEM
A way of cleaning water to make it safe to drink.

WETLAND
Land, such as a swamp or marsh, that is wet most of the time.

WILDFIRE
Fire in the countryside that is hard to put out.

Index